A Clawhammer Christmas

Banjo Solos on Christmas Favorites

by Dan Levenson

I0805601

Online Audio

To access the online audio recording go to:
WWW.MELBAY.COM/30995MEB

Cover image courtesy of Nashville Banjo Company. Figured cherry banjo with 12" rim, goatskin head and red-tail hawk inlay. Hand crafted by Nashville Banjo Company.

WWW.MELBAY.COM

Preface

Merry Christmas! Well at least I hope you will have one by playing these tunes for your friends and family. After all, music makes the season and nothing makes great music more exciting than good old time banjo. It is so reminiscent of the days when the family spent the holidays together to eat, drink, be merry and share the music of the season.

It is with that wish for good family time and good cheer that I present you these clawhammer banjo transcriptions of some of the most well known Christmas carols.

They have been a joy to transcribe (even though it is springtime as I write this). It has often been a challenge for me as well, since these tunes are not your average fiddle tunes for clawhammer banjo. They required some thought about things like playing slower, playing in waltz time (3/4), and even playing some chords I am not familiar with on the banjo. You may find that you too have similar challenges as you start to play the transcriptions for yourself, but do know that all of them are playable by a solid advanced beginner willing to put some time and effort into them.

A couple of things will help you through. Slowing down will likely be the most important thing to remember. These are not dance tunes played at jam speed. (Well, two of them can be.) The other is to get familiar with the fingerboard in each of the three tunings I have used, so you can reach notes that may appear in odd spots. A second fret on the second string instead of an open first string in double-C, or a barred 7th fret or even a 12th-fret chord in G. And the choice to strum a chord, just chord, and/or add or subtract a double or drop-thumbed note when you choose. Or even make the tune follow a bit different melody as YOU remember it.

To those points, I have written all of the tunes here in either G, double C or what we call G modal tuning. With those three tunings you can easily capo up to your preferred key (usually the one you or your family sing in). My choice for which tuning to use for each tune was dependent upon how the fingering best laid out on the banjo in order to make it as easy as possible to play. A couple of the songs, "Jingle Bells" and "We Wish You a Merry Christmas" played well in both G and double-C tuning, so I have transcribed them in both.

To me, what makes a five-string banjo unique is that fifth string, and what makes clawhammer ring out is the use of the fifth string AND the use of drop thumb to give it that distinct banjo sound. So, I have written the tunes with a lot of double and drop-thumb and in the case of a tune like "Jingle Bells", I think that really adds to the feel of the tune. To me, this is what clawhammer banjo is all about. The only unique symbol in the tab in this book may be the note with the square box around it. That is a half note and takes 2 beats. I only used it at the end of a couple of tunes so just play it and let it ring. Otherwise, the tab is pretty much as it is in all of my books.

Some of you may not be ready for so much double and drop yet, or feel differently about the use of that thumb. In that case, your judgment is as good as anyone's and as long as you like the sound of it your way, play it your way. Leave out some of the drop-thumbs or other backbeats. Pick a rhythmic strum that best backs your singing. Make it your own and enjoy the journey. My tabs are meant to be a guide to get you started. You will turn the notes on the pages into music to be enjoyed by all. AND, just BTW, if you feel you (or a friend or family member) wants to improve their clawhammer skills, check out my book, *Clawhammer Banjo From Scratch* (MB 20190M) for a complete instruction manual including these techniques and more.

About the recordings: Be aware, my recordings are not exactly as tabbed. And, they are here for you *au naturel*. That means that they are not fancy or slick. I will stay close to the tab, but there will be some variations from what is printed. That is by intent. I consider the differences between them variations and they add to your list of possibilities when playing the tunes for yourself. There may be more drop-thumbs or less, double-thumb where a quarter note is written and vice-versa. You should feel free to take liberties; I did. All of the tracks were recorded with a 12-inch pot, cherry 25 1/2" scale banjo from the Nashville Banjo Company.

For me, this year will be a double-thumb drop-thumb Christmas. May you and yours be healthy and joyous in this special season for all humankind. Merry Christmas, Happy Channukah, Joyous Kwanza, Good Yule, Happy Festivus and a safe and healthy New Year! Play well and ...

Play Nice,
Dan Levenson – April 2021
www.Clawdan.com

Contents

Angels We Have Heard on High

1

G Tuning
gDGBD

Away in a Manger

G Tuning
gDGBD

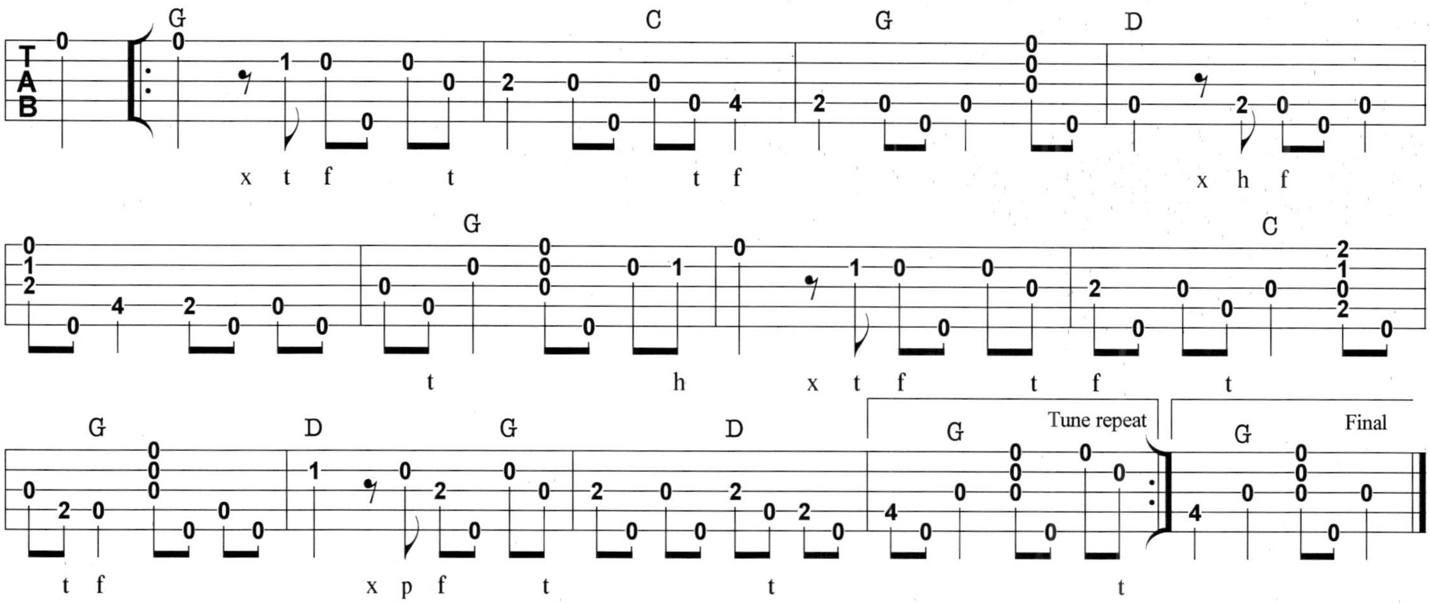

Breakin' Up Christmas

G Tuning
gDGBD

Breakin' Up Christmas refers to "Old Christmas" which is still celebrated in the Appalachian mountains.

It is a popular fiddle tune and usually played in A. I have written this out in G tuning with the key of G chords noted but it is usually played in A. To get there, tune to G tuning as noted and put your capo on the second fret; then, tune or capo your fifth string up to A or you can tune the banjo up to aEAC♯E. Likewise, your chords would reflect the Key of A if you are playing it at that pitch. G becomes A, C becomes D and D becomes E.

The second part has lyrics, though they might have been added later.

Santa Claus has come and gone
Breaking up Christmas all night long...

Children Go Where I Send Thee

G Tuning
gDGBD

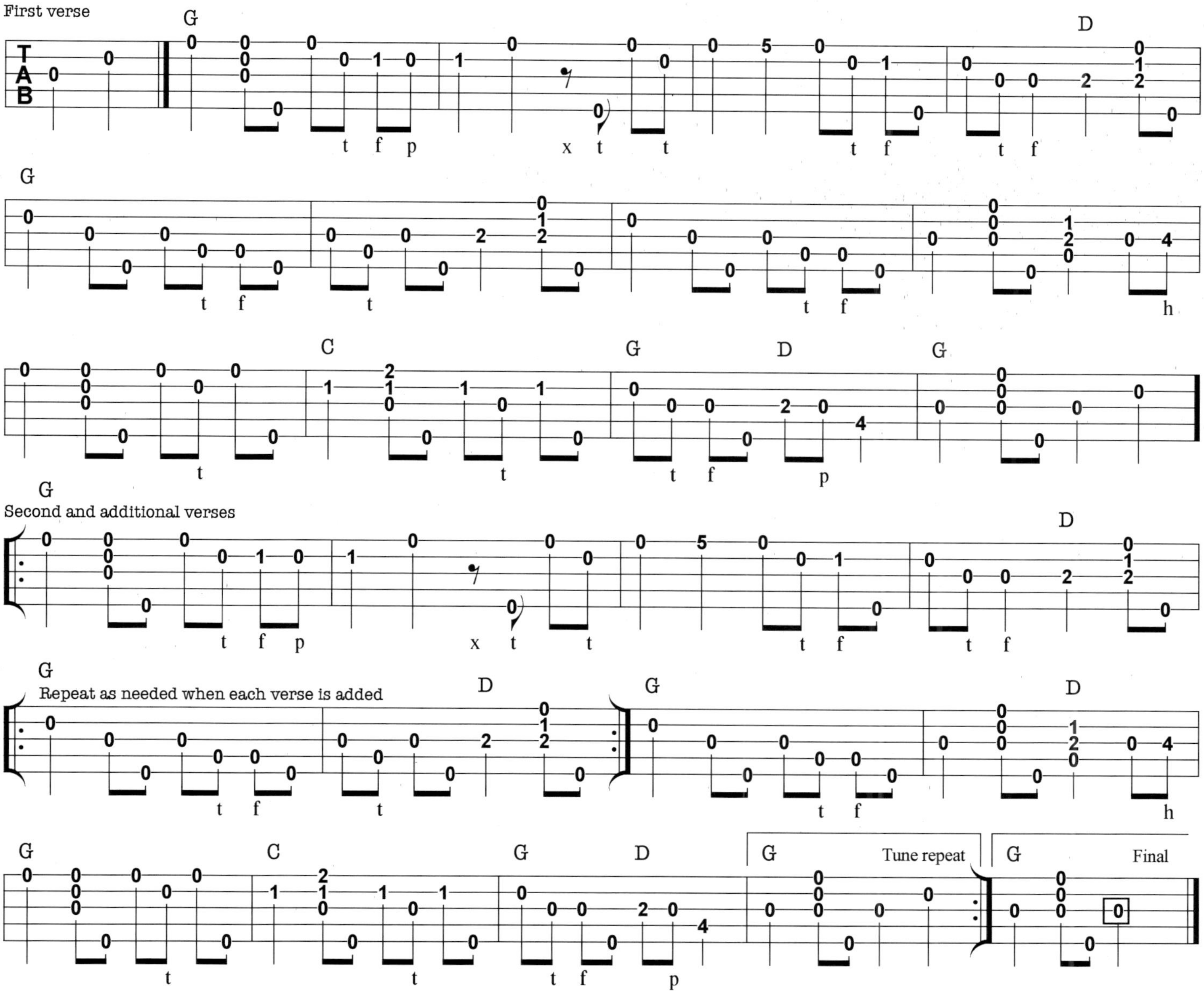

This song can look confusing. In the first verse, the lyrics are:
"Children go where I send thee (you), How shall I send you? I'm going to send you one by one,
One for the little-bitty baby who was born, born, born in Bethlehem."

The second and subsequent verses add a "destination" each time but still end with, "One for the little-bitty baby who was..." So, each time you add a verse, you repeat the two measures in line 5. The first time (actually the second verse) you do NOT repeat it with "Two for Paul and Silas" then on to "One for ..."

In the third and subsequent verses, you repeat those measures as needed:
"Three for the Hebrew Children, Two for Paul and Silas, One for the little-bitty baby ..."

The last time through, you will repeat it 11 times for: "Twelve for the Twelve Apostles,
Eleven for eleven deriders, Ten for the Ten Commandments, Nine for the nine all dressed so fine,
Eight for the eight that stood at the gate, Seven for the seven that never got to heaven,
Six for the six that couldn't get fixed, Five for the five that couldn't get by, Four for the four that stood at the door, Three for the Hebrew children, Two by two for Paul and Silas,
One for the little-bitty baby, who was born, born, born in Bethlehem"

Christmas Eve

Double-C Tuning
gCGCD

This is the tune played and recorded by Uncle Dick Hutchison of Disney, OK and by The Wolfe Brothers from Grayson County, VA. There are a lot of tunes with this name as well as "Christmas Day" and "Christmas Morning" or "Christmas Morn".

I wrote this tune out in double-C tuning, even though Uncle Dick played this one in D. It is not uncommon to repitch tune keys according to your voice and you should do that if you want to sing the words as you and the Wolfe Brothers played it in about C♯; so capo up 1 or 2 frets to play it as they did.

And, there are lyrics. Here are the ones that The Wolfe Brothers sing:

a part:
1 - Wintertime in Grayson county; Didn't have much spending bounty
Old folks said if you believe; You'll get a gift on Christmas Eve.

b part:
"Hee hee" the children say; Come on Santa head this way
Hee hee we believe; That you'll be here on Christmas Eve.

2 - Then came the dawn so white and pearly; We were up so bright and early
We could hardly scarely believe; The things we got on Christmas Eve

Hee hee...

3- Brand new dress for Pretty Polly; Cheslie got a brand new dolly,
Santa hid it up his sleeve; And left it here on Christmas Eve.

Deck the Halls

G Tuning
gDGBD

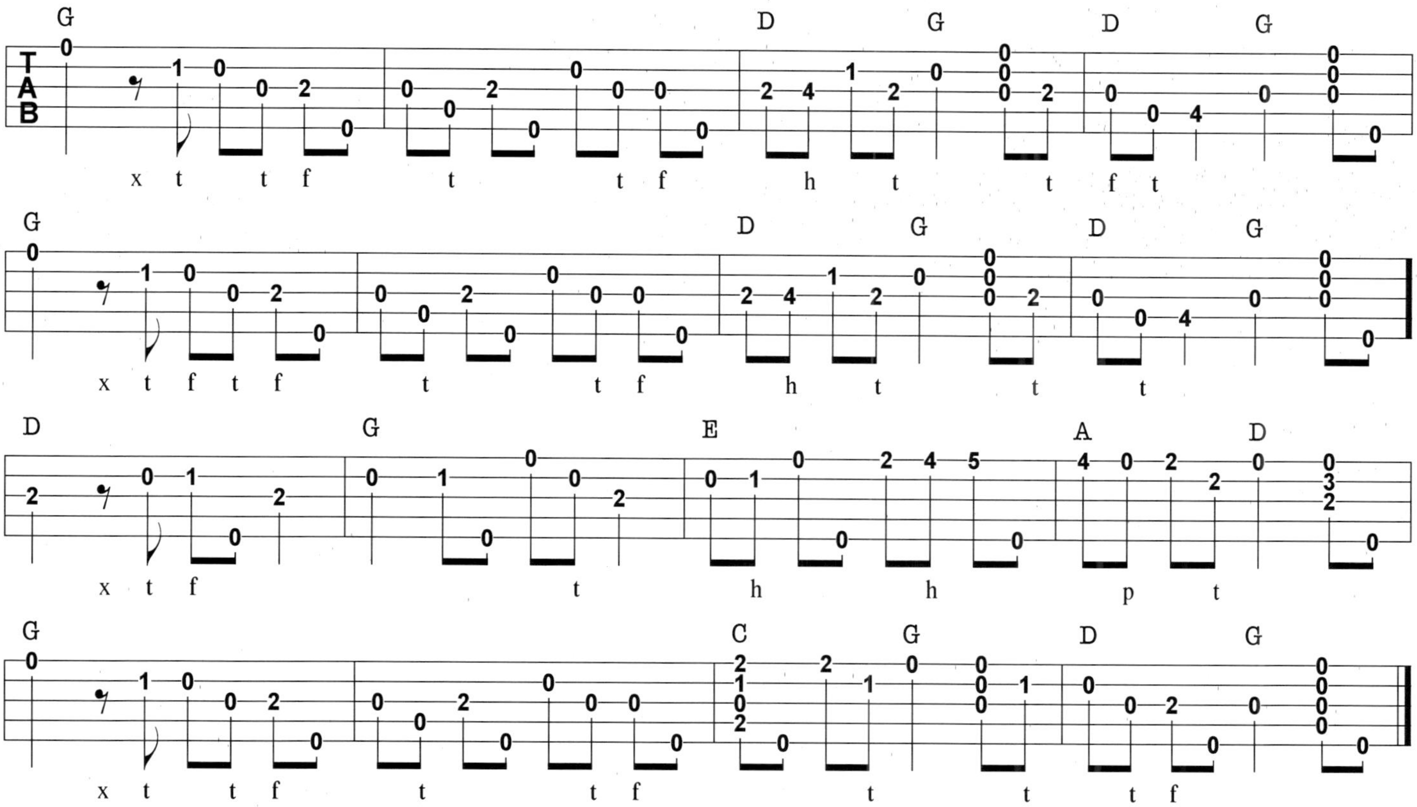

The First Noel

7

G Tuning
gDGBD

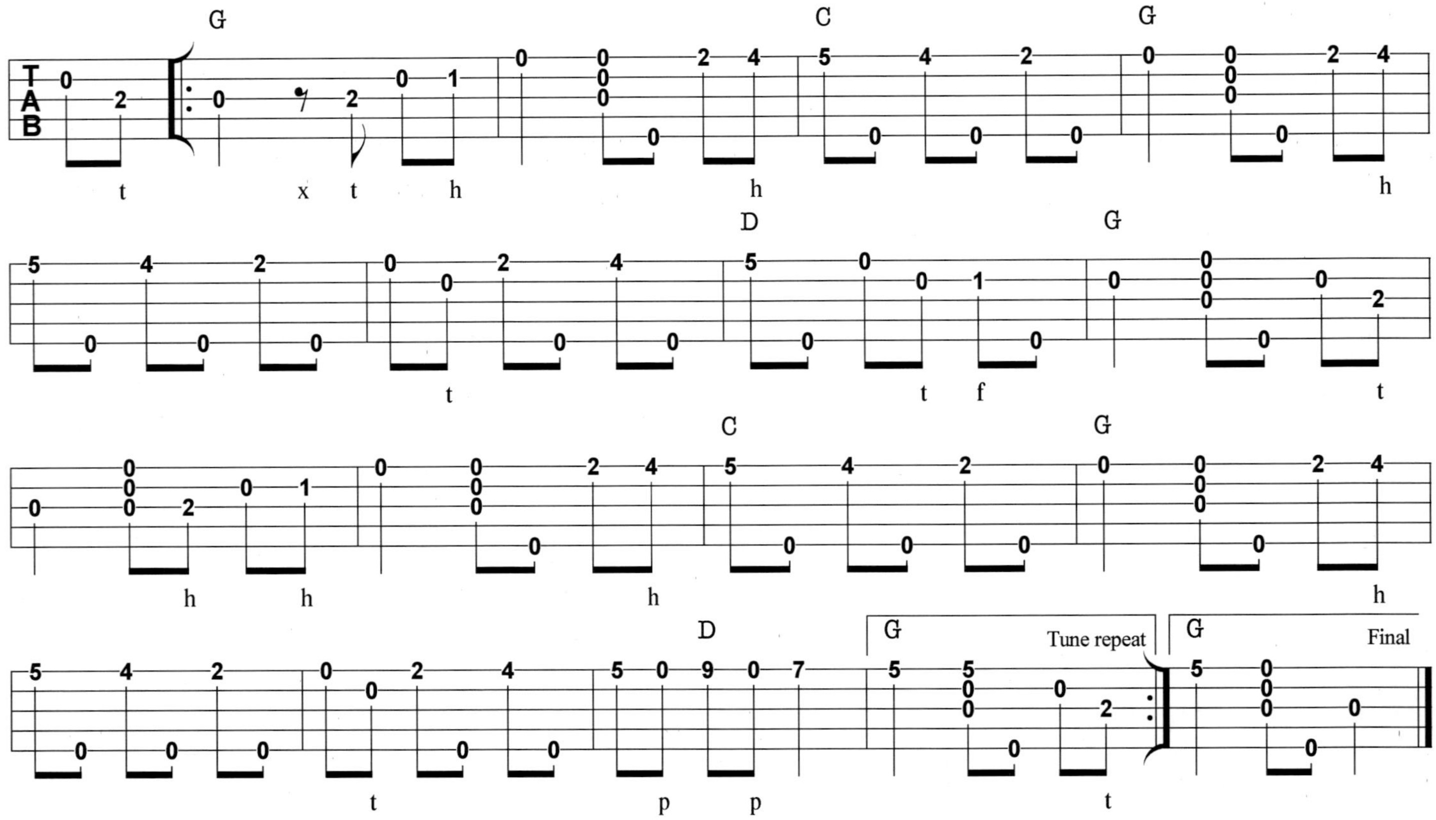

Go Tell It on the Mountain

G Tuning
gDGBD

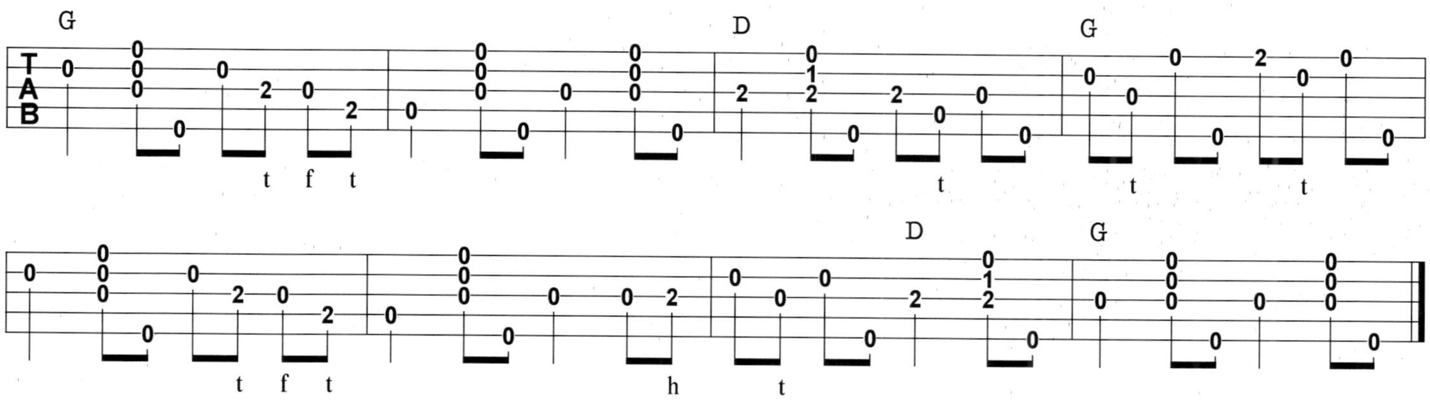

Go, tell it on the mountain
Over the hills and everywhere
Go, tell it on the mountain
That Jesus Christ is born

While shepherds kept their watching
O'er silent flocks by night
Behold throughout the heavens
There shone a Holy light

Go, tell it on the mountain
Over the hills and everywhere
Go, tell it on the mountain
That Jesus Christ is born

The shepherds feared and trembled
When, lo! Above the earth
Rang out the angel chorus
That hailed our Savior's birth

Go, tell it on the mountain
Over the hills and everywhere
Go, tell it on the mountain
That Jesus Christ is born

Down in a lowly manger
Our humble Christ was born
And brought us all salvation
That blessed Christmas morn

Go, tell it on the mountain
Over the hills and everywhere
Go, tell it on the mountain
That Jesus Christ is born
That Jesus Christ is born

9

God Rest Ye Merry, Gentlemen

G Tuning
gDGBD

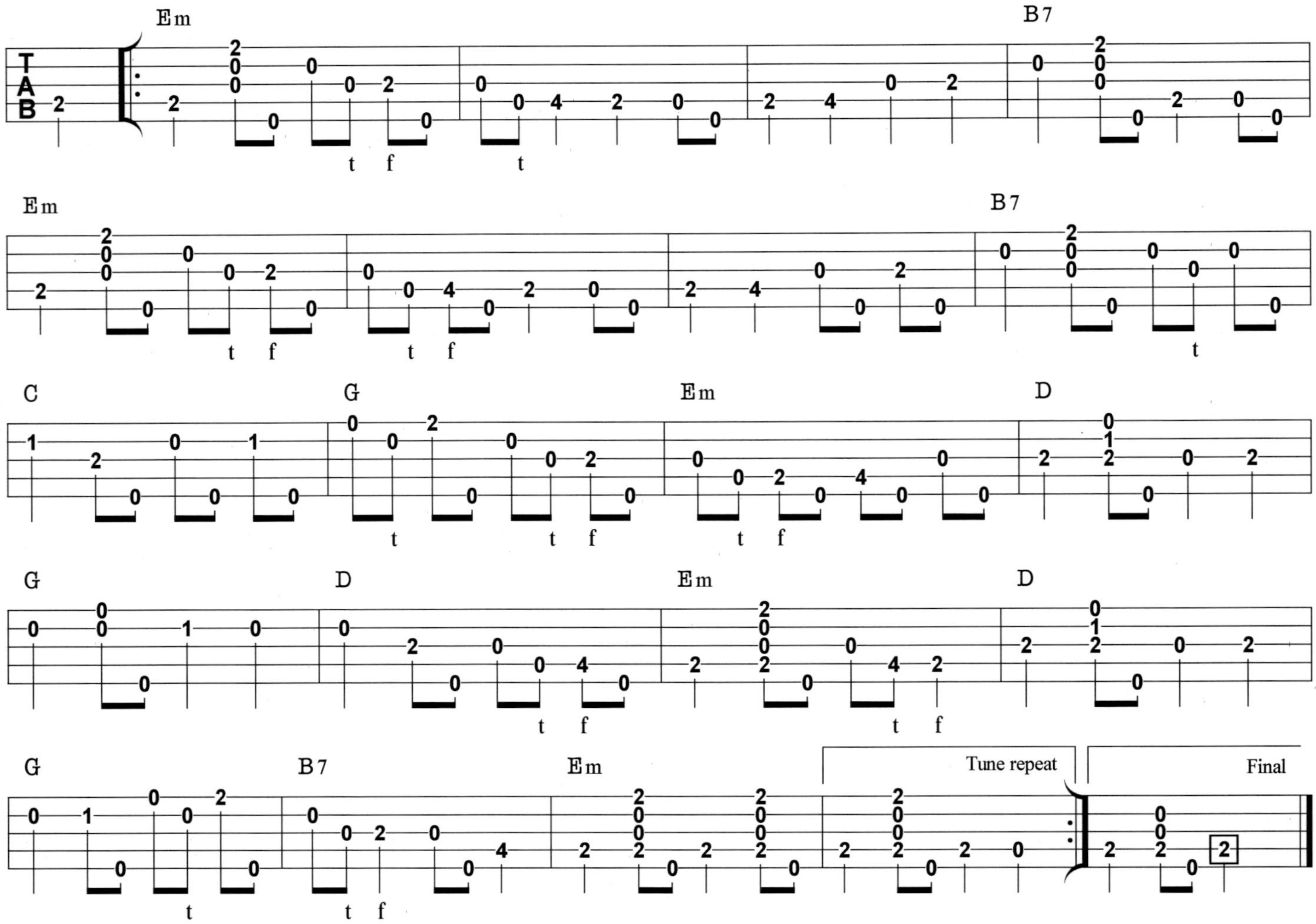

Good King Wenceslas

10

G Tuning
gDGBD

Hark! The Herald Angels Sing

G Tuning
gDGBD

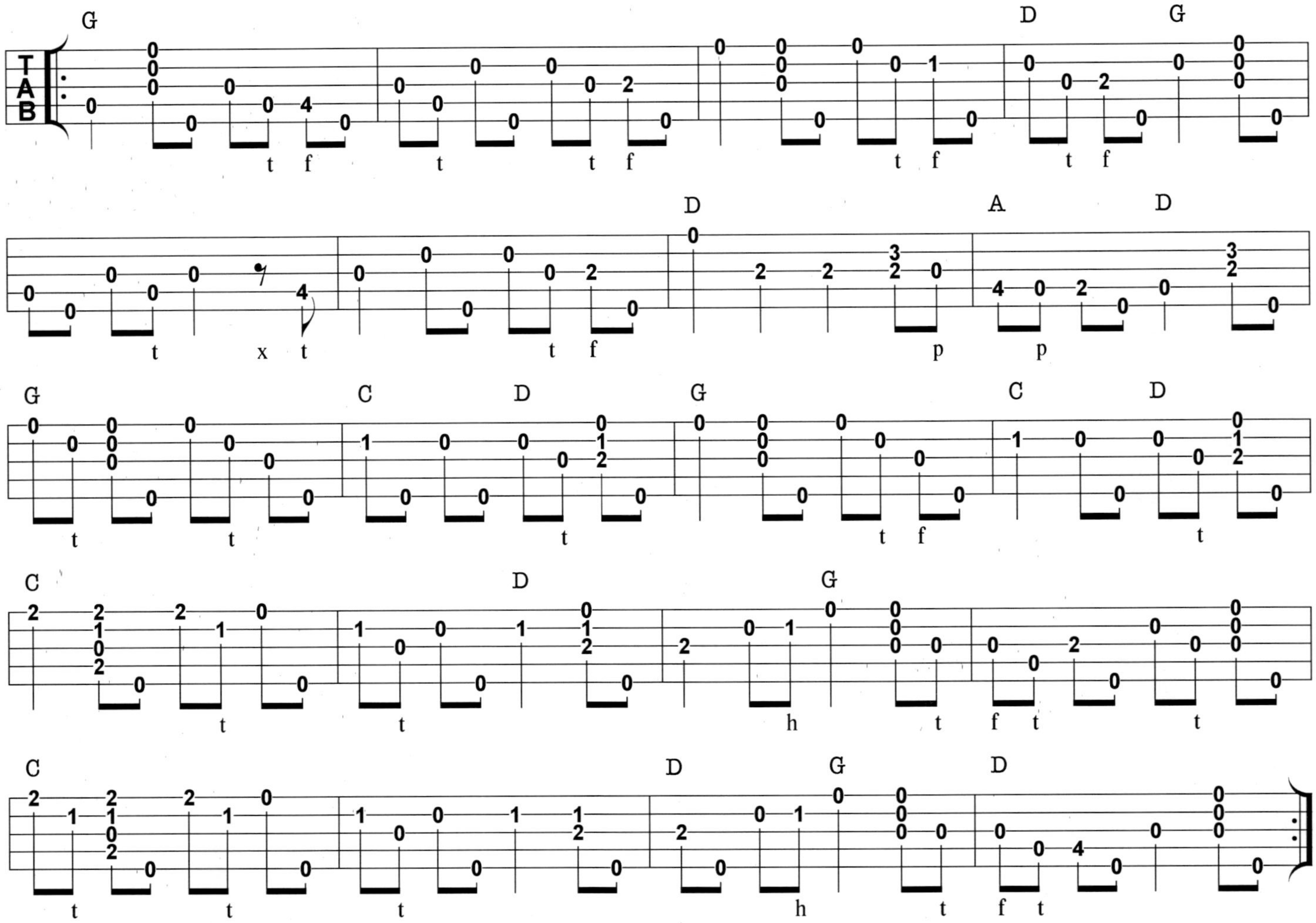

The Holly and the Ivy

12

G Tuning
gDGBD

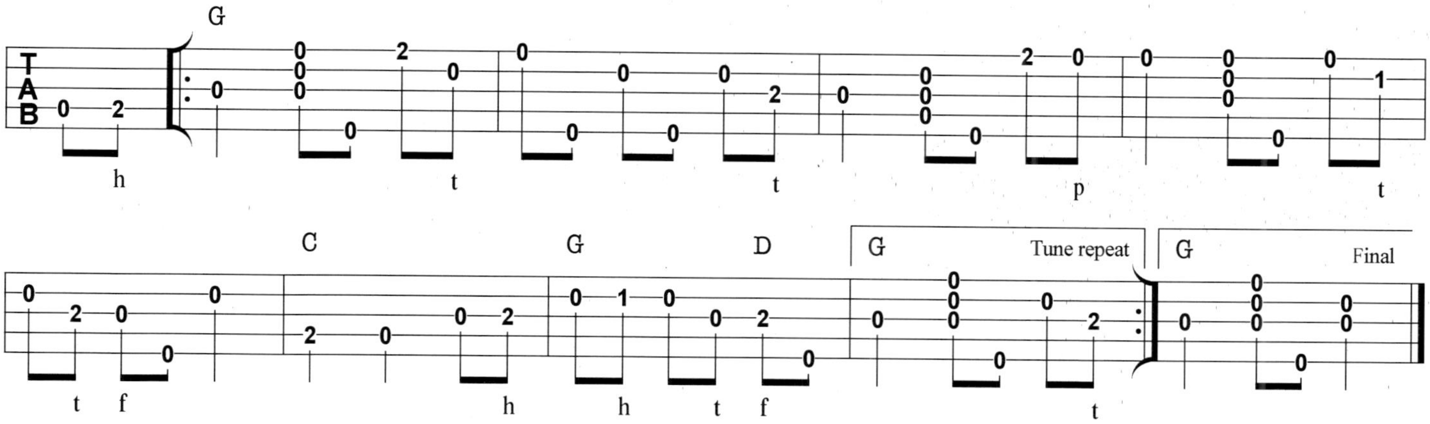

Modern lyrics:

The holly and the ivy
When they are both full grown
Of all trees that are in the wood
The holly bears the crown
O, the rising of the sun
And the running of the deer
The playing of the merry organ
Sweet singing in the choir

The holly bears a blossom
As white as lily flow'r
And Mary bore sweet Jesus Christ
To be our dear Saviour
O, the rising of the sun
And the running of the deer
The playing of the merry organ
Sweet singing in the choir

The holly bears a berry
As red as any blood
And Mary bore sweet Jesus Christ
To do poor sinners good
O, the rising of the sun
And the running of the deer
The playing of the merry organ
Sweet singing in the choir

The holly bears a prickle
As sharp as any thorn
And Mary bore sweet Jesus Christ
On Christmas Day in the morn
O, the rising of the sun
And the running of the deer
The playing of the merry organ
Sweet singing in the choir

The holly bears a bark
As bitter as any gall
And Mary bore sweet Jesus Christ
For to redeem us all
O, the rising of the sun
And the running of the deer
The playing of the merry organ
Sweet singing in
Sweet singing in
In the choir

Earlier lyrics:

Holly stands in the hall, fair to behold:
Ivy stands without the door, she is full sore a cold.
Nay, ivy, nay, it shall not be I wis;
Let holly have the mastery, as the manner is.

Holly and his merry men, they dance and they sing,
Ivy and her maidens, they weep and they wring.
Nay, ivy, nay, it shall not be I wis;
Let holly have the mastery, as the manner is.

Ivy hath chapped fingers, she caught them from the cold,
So might they all have, aye, that with ivy hold.
Nay, ivy, nay, it shall not be I wis;
Let holly have the mastery, as the manner is.

Holly hath berries red as any rose,
The forester, the hunter, keep them from the does.
Nay, ivy, nay, it shall not be I wis;
Let holly have the mastery, as the manner is.

Ivy hath berries black as any sloe;
There come the owl and eat him as she go.
Nay, ivy, nay, it shall not be I wis;
Let holly have the mastery, as the manner is.

Holly hath birds a fair full flock,
The nightingale, the popinjay, the gentle laverock.
Nay, ivy, nay, it shall not be I wis;
Let holly have the mastery, as the manner is.

Good ivy, what birds hast thou?
None but the owlet that cries how, how.
Nay, ivy, nay, it shall not be I wis;
Let holly have the mastery, as the manner is.

It Came Upon the Midnight Clear

13

G Tuning
gDGBD

14

Jingle Bells
(in C)

Double-C Tuning
gCGCD

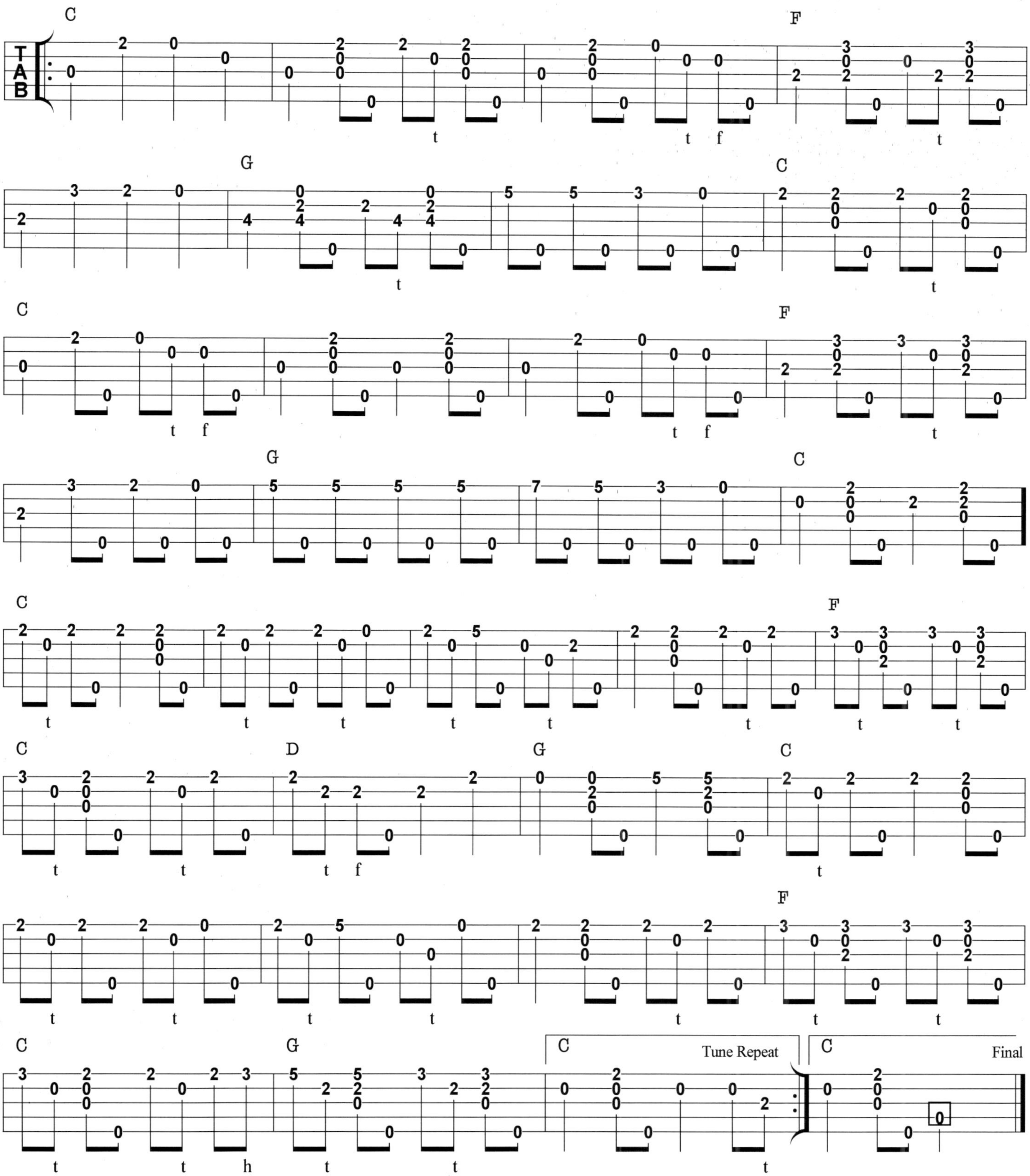

This tune works well in both double-C tuning and G tuning, so both tabbed-out keys are in this book. I think the double and drop thumb makes it sound like the jingle bells!

Jingle Bells
(in G)

15

G Tuning
gDGBD

For the A chord (line 6, measure 3), just bar across all of the strings at the second fret.

Joy to the World

16

G Tuning
gDGBD

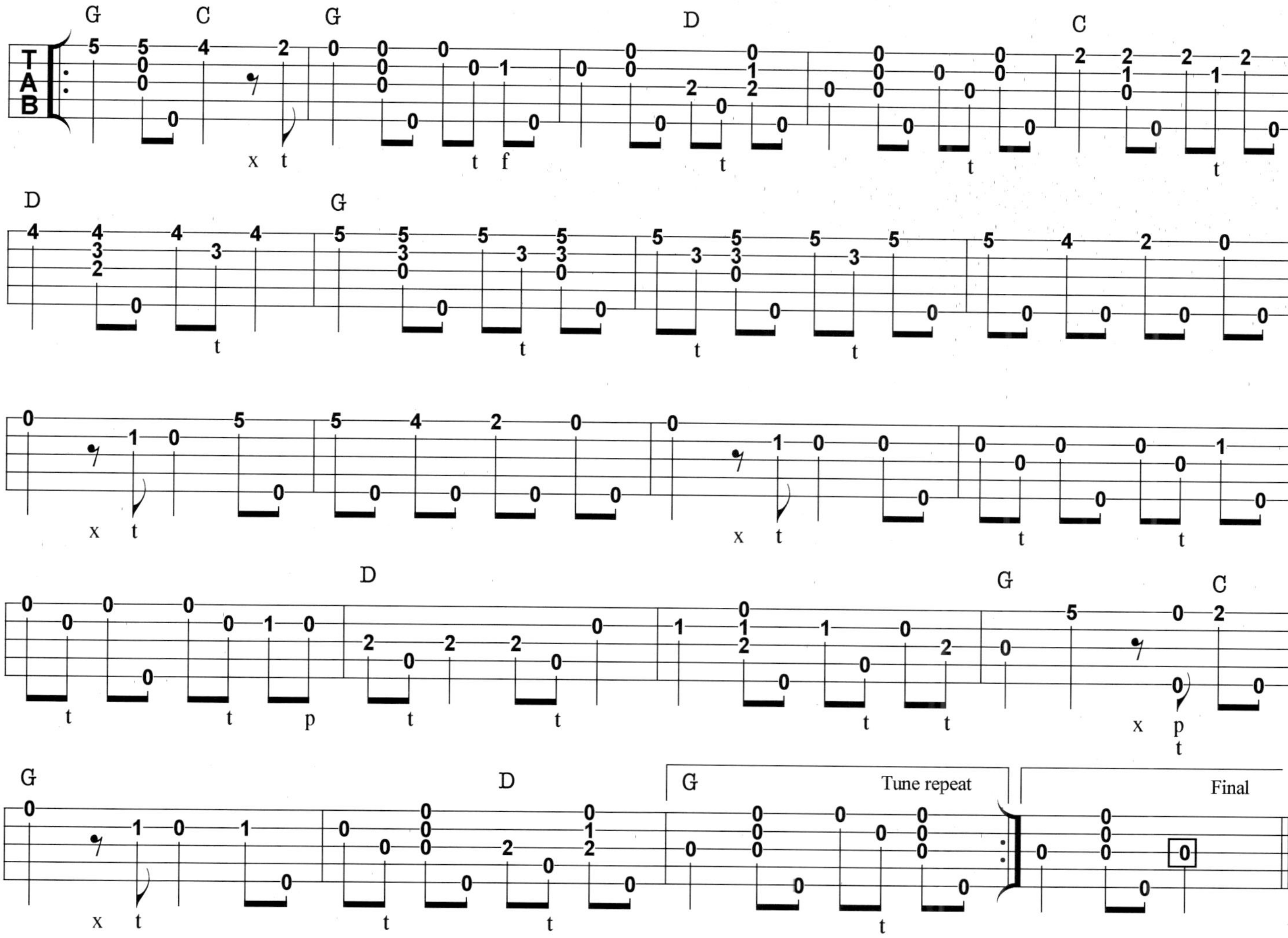

Yes, in the last measure of line 4, that is a pull-off and a thumbed 5th string at the same time. Feel free to just do one or the other if you find it confusing, or just prefer it that way.

O Come, All Ye Faithful

17

Double-C Tuning
gCGCD

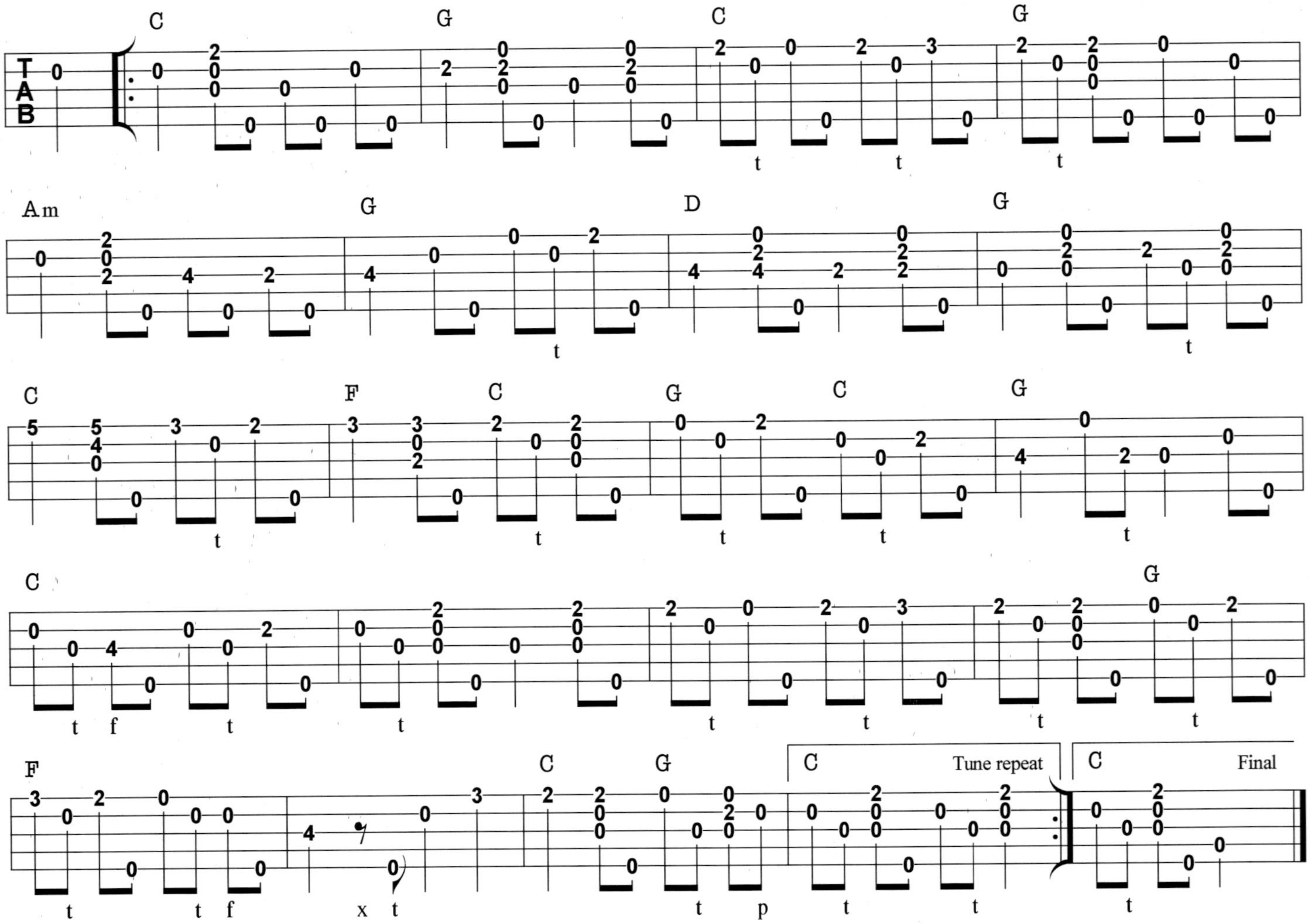

18

O Little Town of Bethlehem

G Tuning
gDGBD

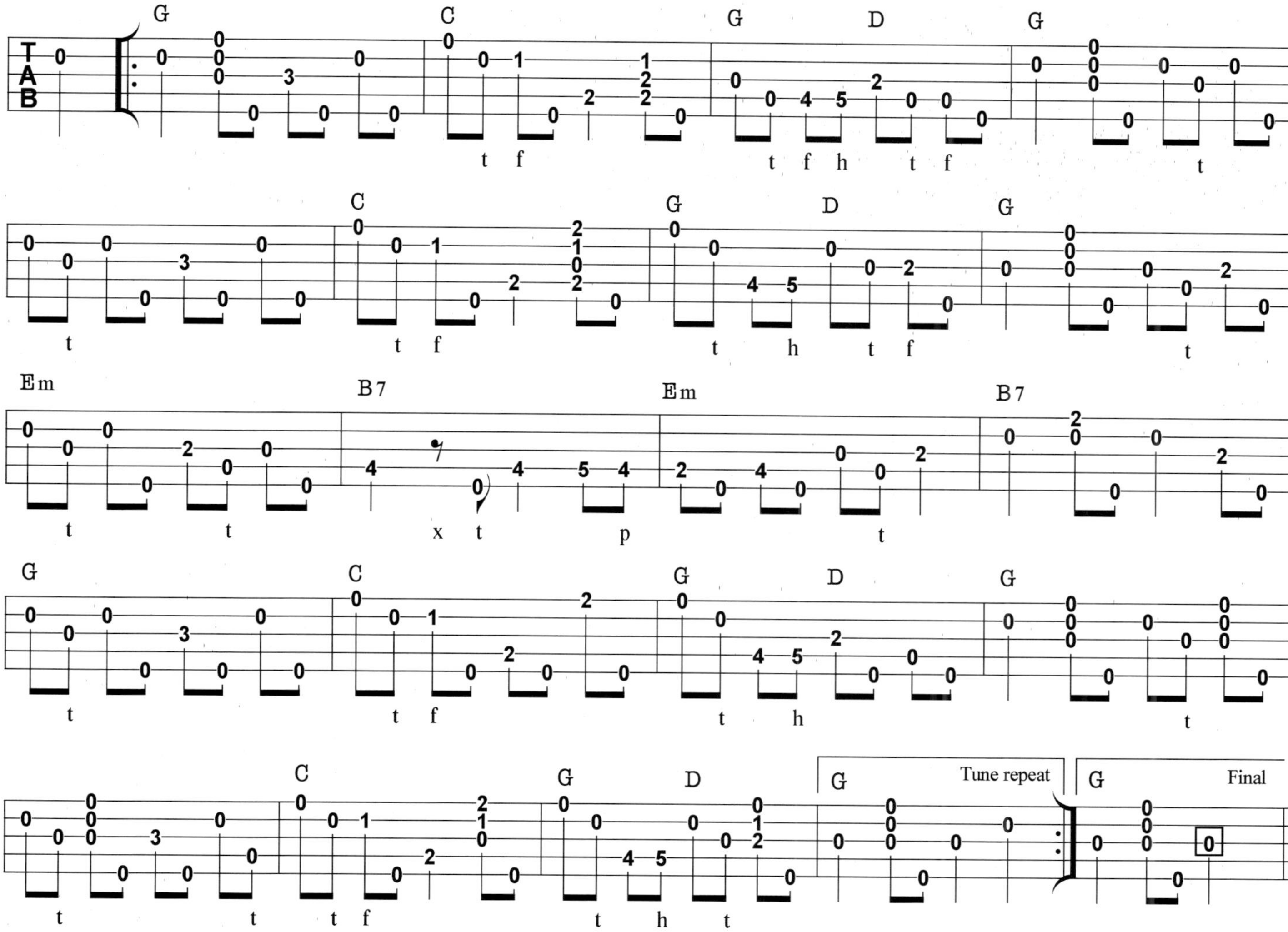

O Holy Night

19

G Tuning
gDGBD

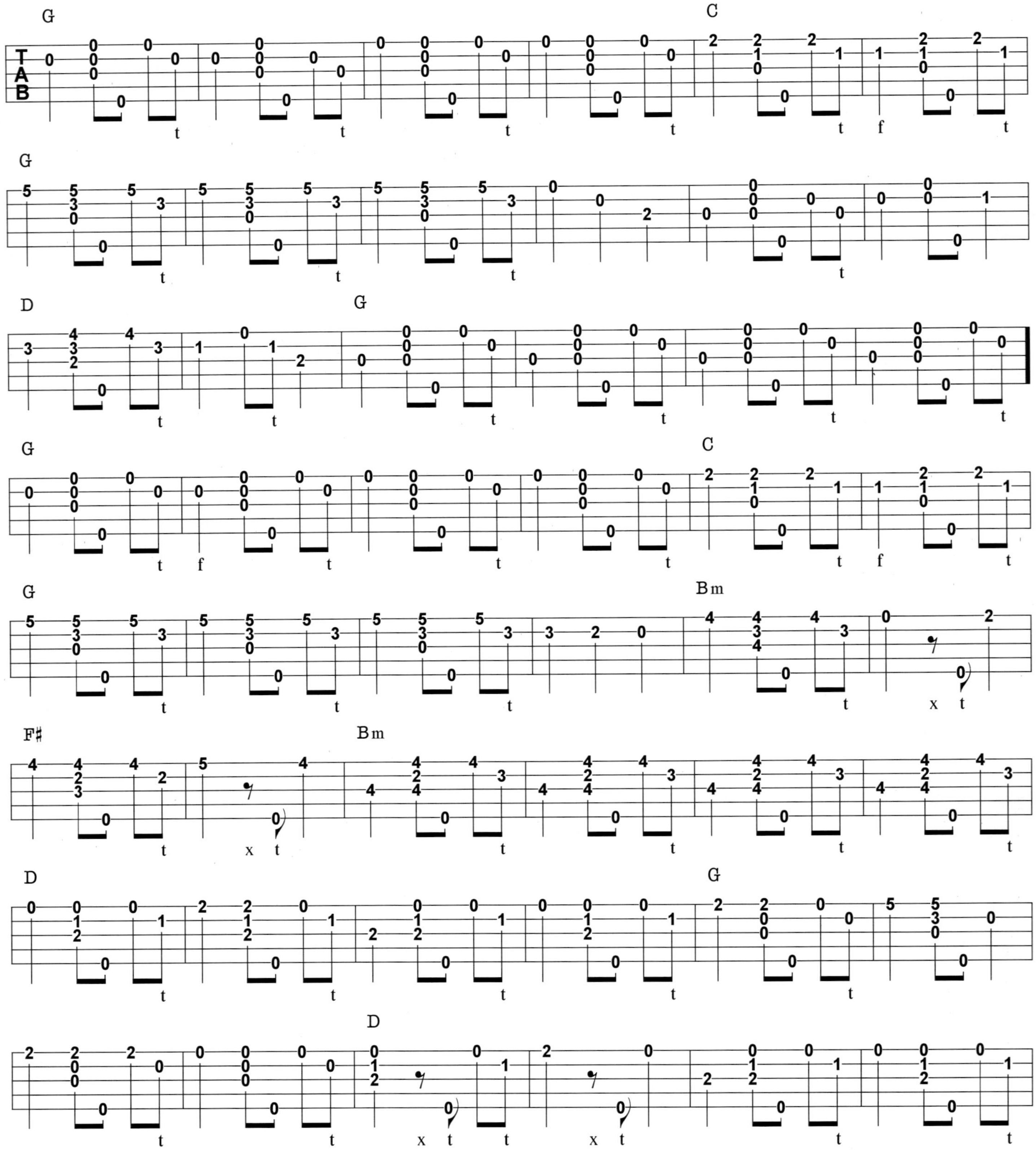

This is probably the most difficult tune in this book, both because of the slow timing AND the upper fret work towards the end. If you are patient and can take the time to break down each part, you should be able to play it just as written. Feel free to play those chords at a lower part of the neck if you prefer.

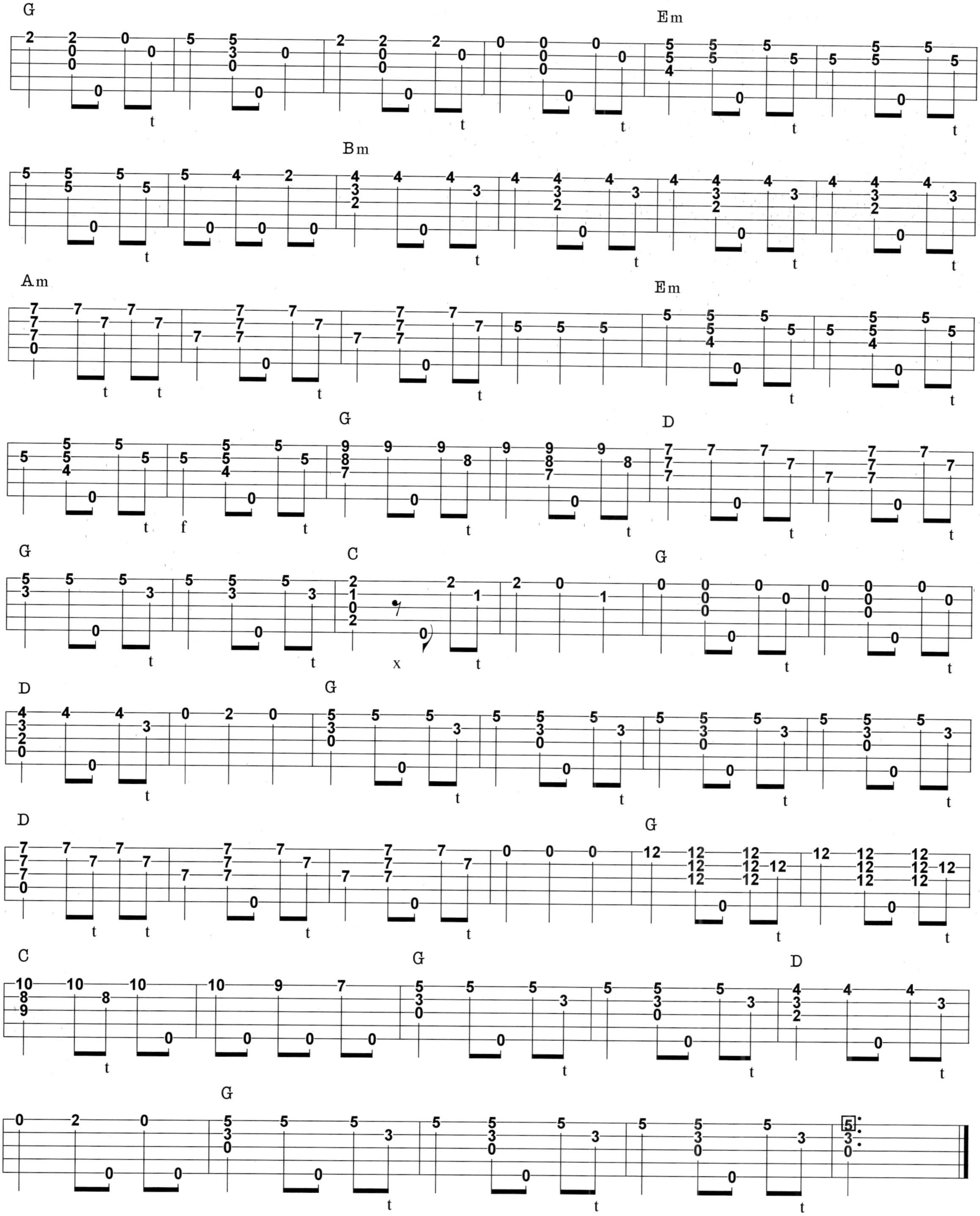
G
Em
Bm
Am
Em
G
D
G
C
G
D
G
D
G
C
G
D
G

O Tannenbaum
(O Christmas Tree)

20

Double-C Tuning
gCGCD

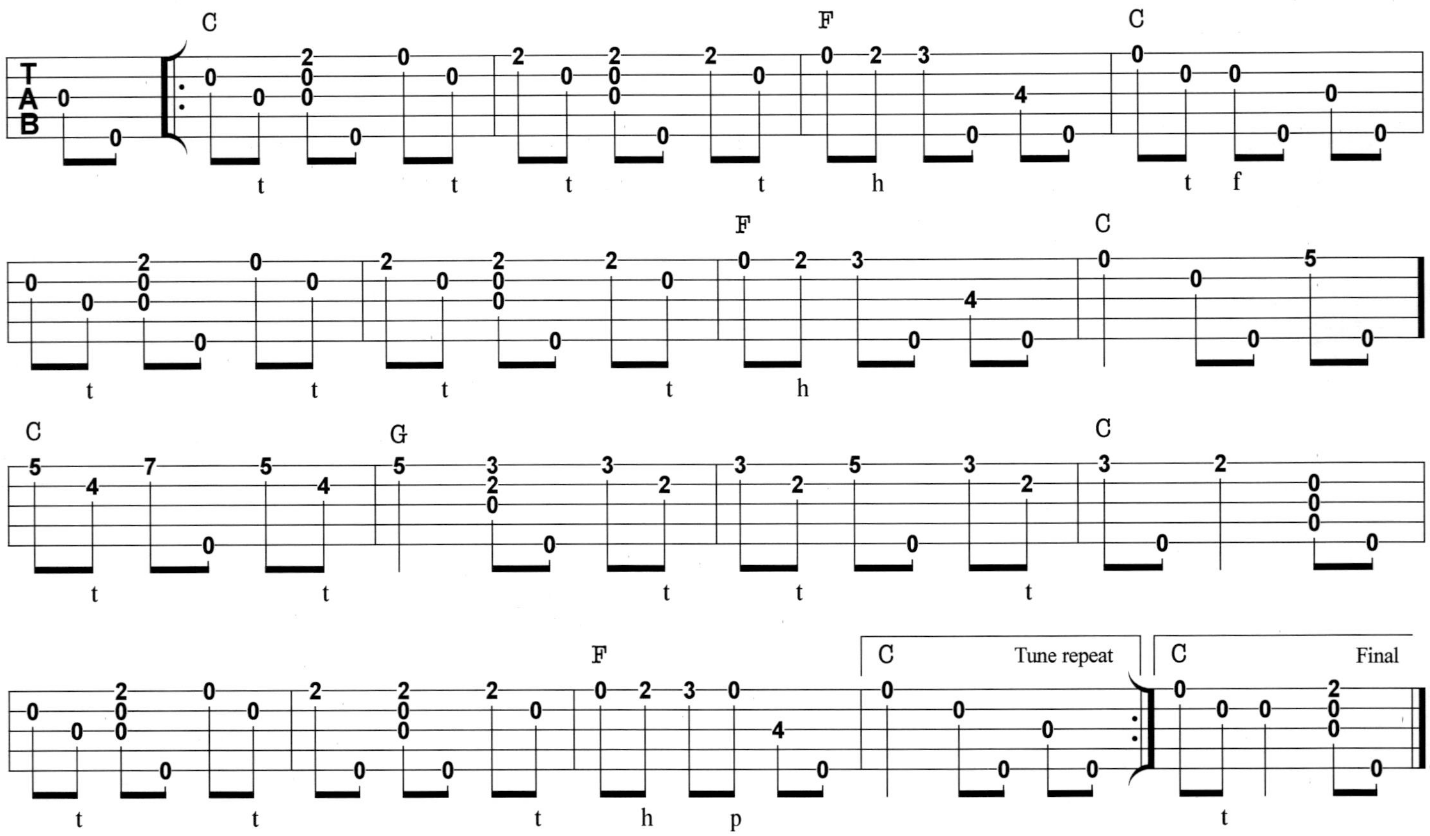

For those who are wondering, "Tannenbaum" is German for "fir tree".

In the first measure of the third line, I suggest you place your index finger on the 4th fret of the second string and your middle finger on the 5th fret of the first string; then, use your pinky to hit the 7th-fret note while keeping your other two fingers in place.

21

I Saw Three Ships on Christmas Day

Double-C Tuning
gCGCD

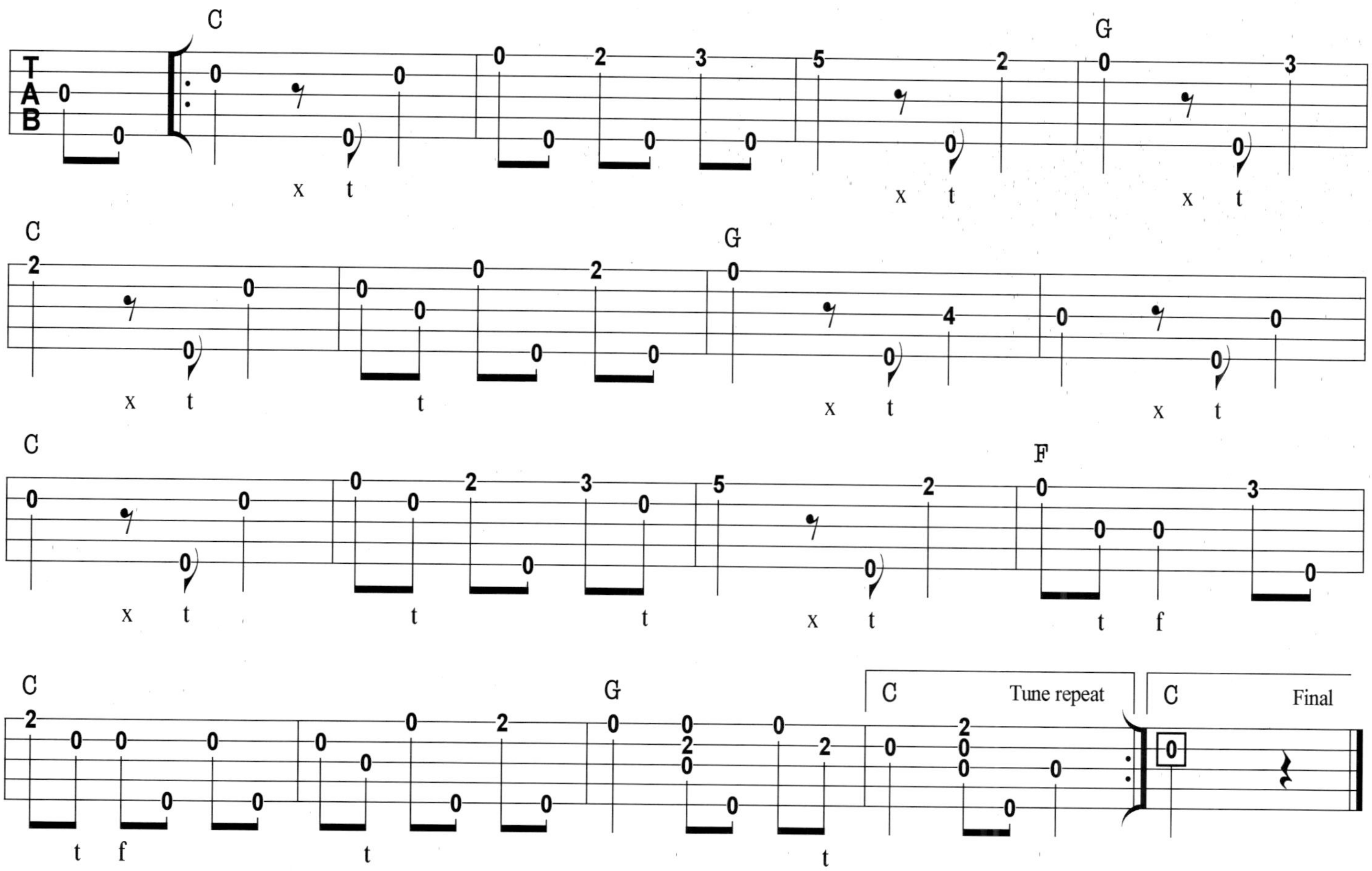

22

Sussex Carol

G Tuning
gDGBD

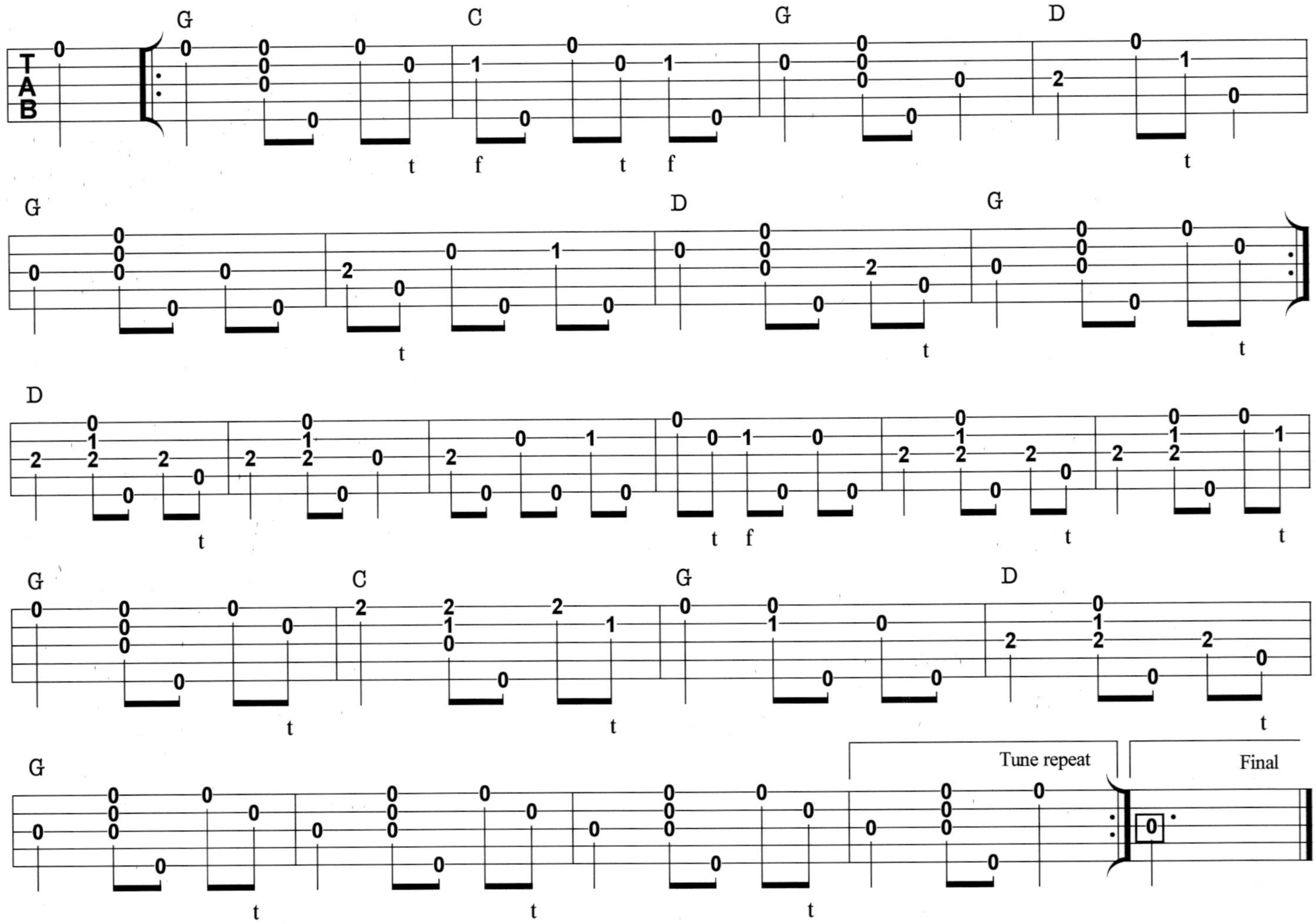

23

Silent Night

Double-C Tuning
gCGCD

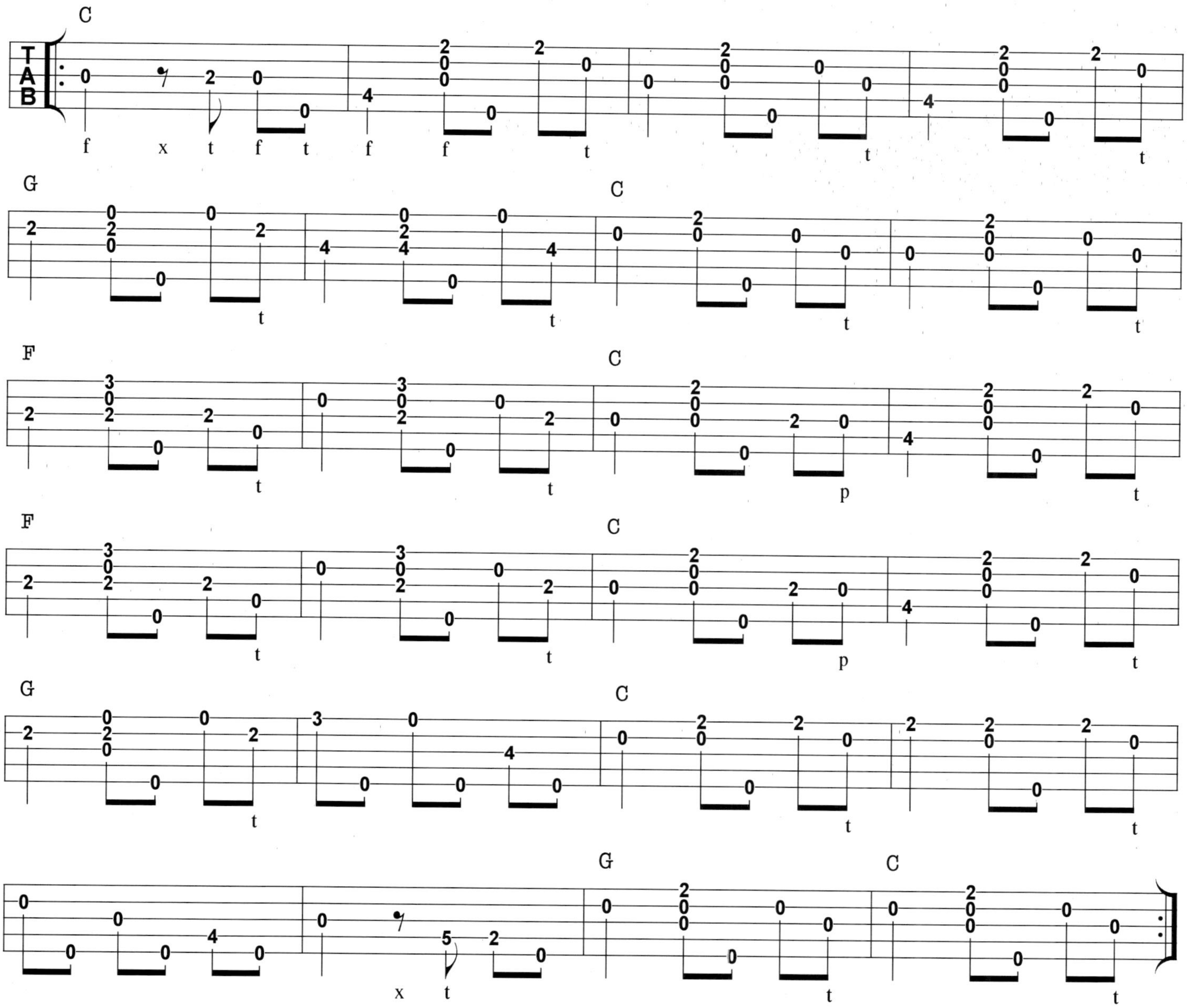

Toyland

24

G Tuning
gDGBD

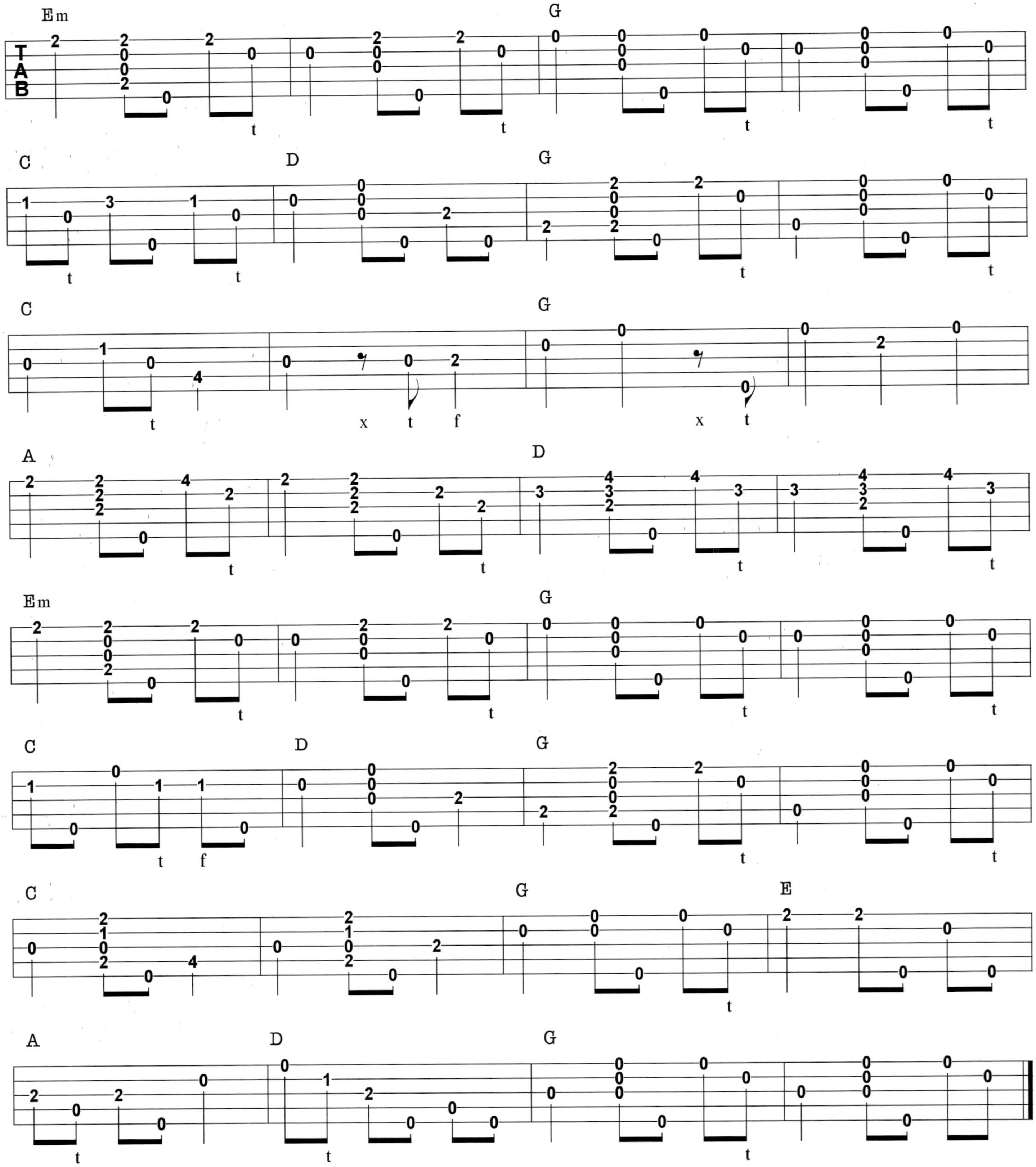

25

We Three Kings

G-Modal Tuning
gDGCD

Twelve Days of Christmas

26

G Tuning
gDGBD

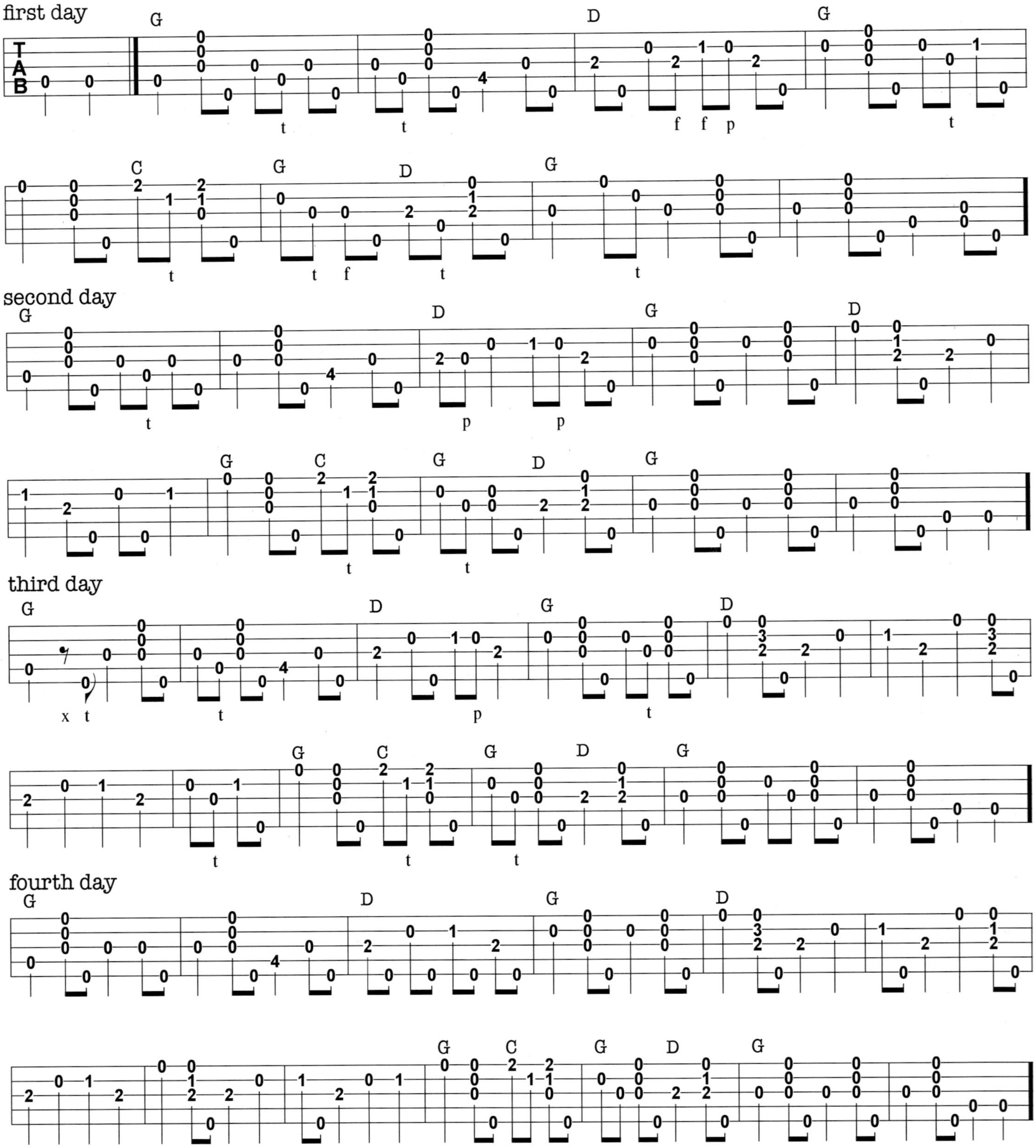

fifth day

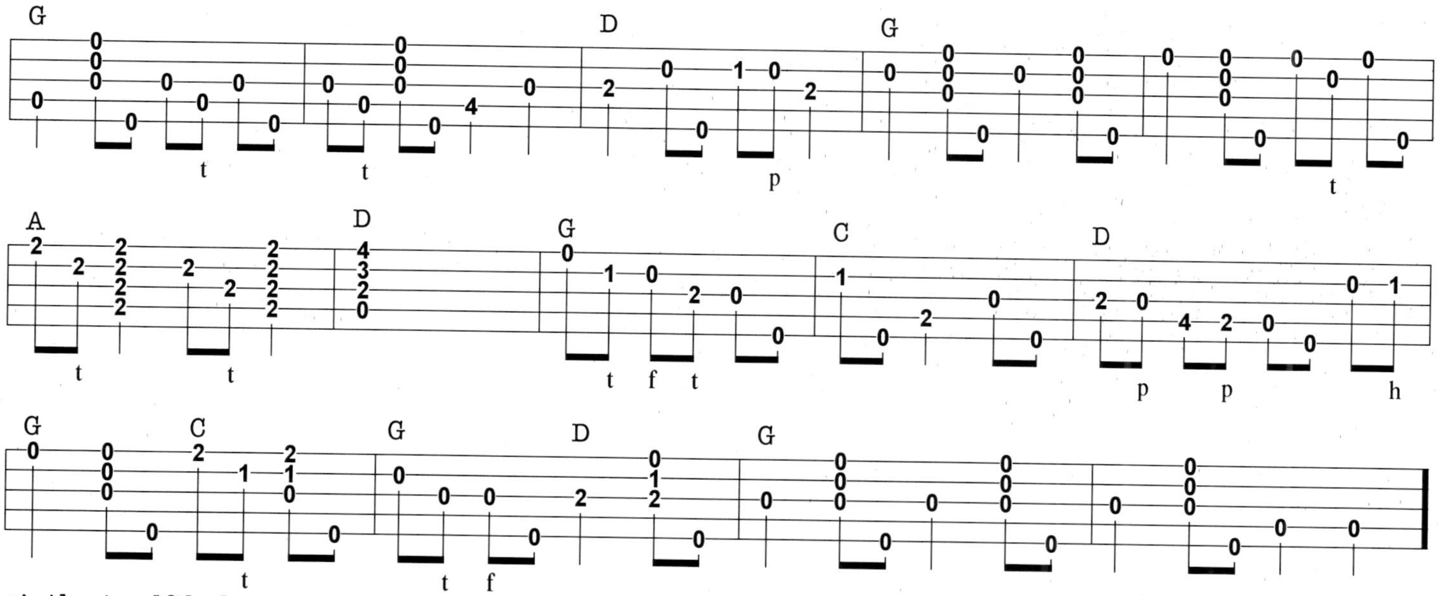

sixth - twelfth day

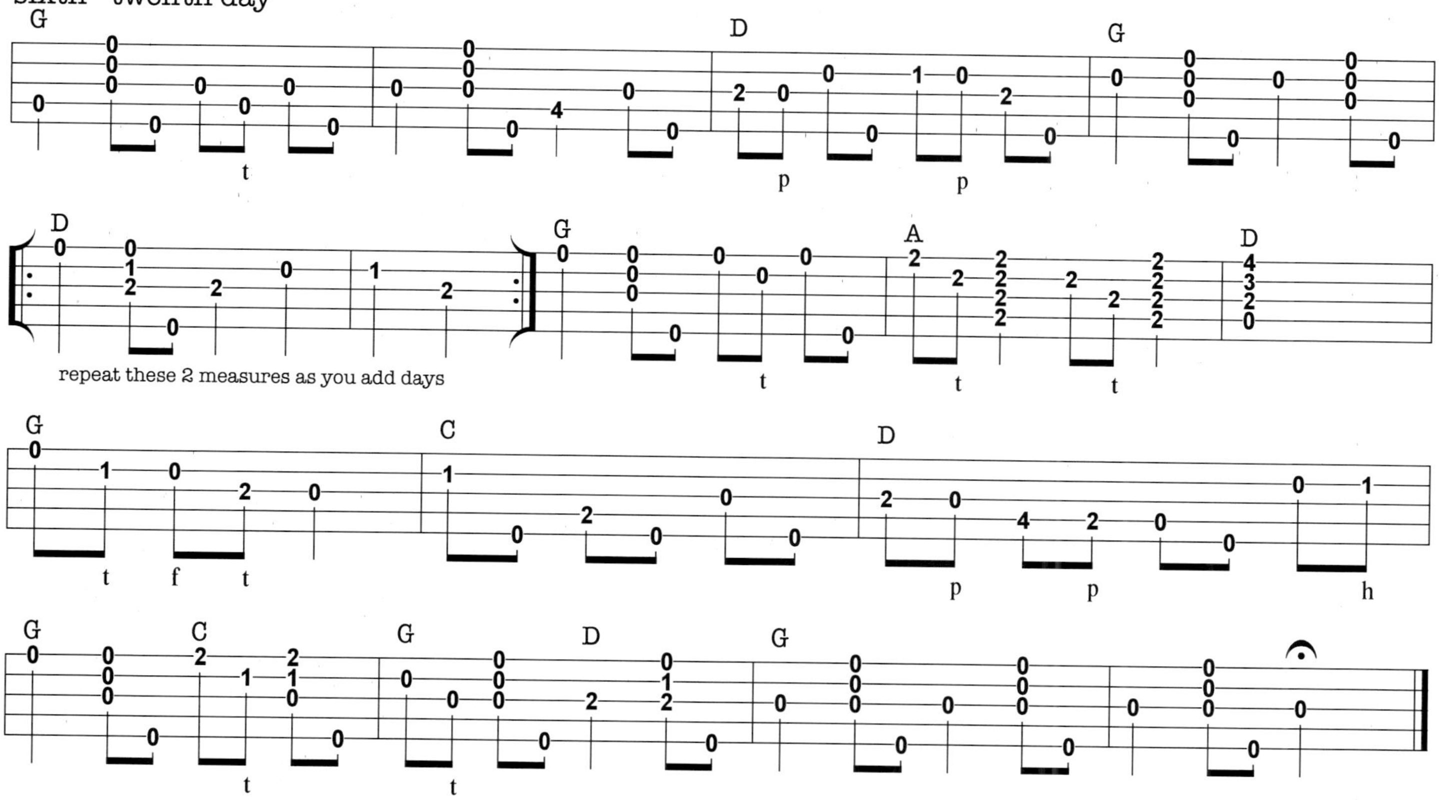

This song is an interesting one to write. Each verse is different until the 6th-12th, so depend on your memory of the tune to get the timing and parts right. I drag out the last day each time, but feel free to time it as you wish.

Then, there are all of those second-fret notes for "Gold" on those "Gold Rings". I bar those notes with my index finger, to hold it all down for the drop thumbs and strums. It isn't hard, but it may seem awkward if you have never done it before.

All in all, a bit of a challenge to play, but not that difficult and such a sense of accomplishment once you have all of those gifts!

27

We Wish You a Merry Christmas

(in C)

Double-C Tuning
gCGCD

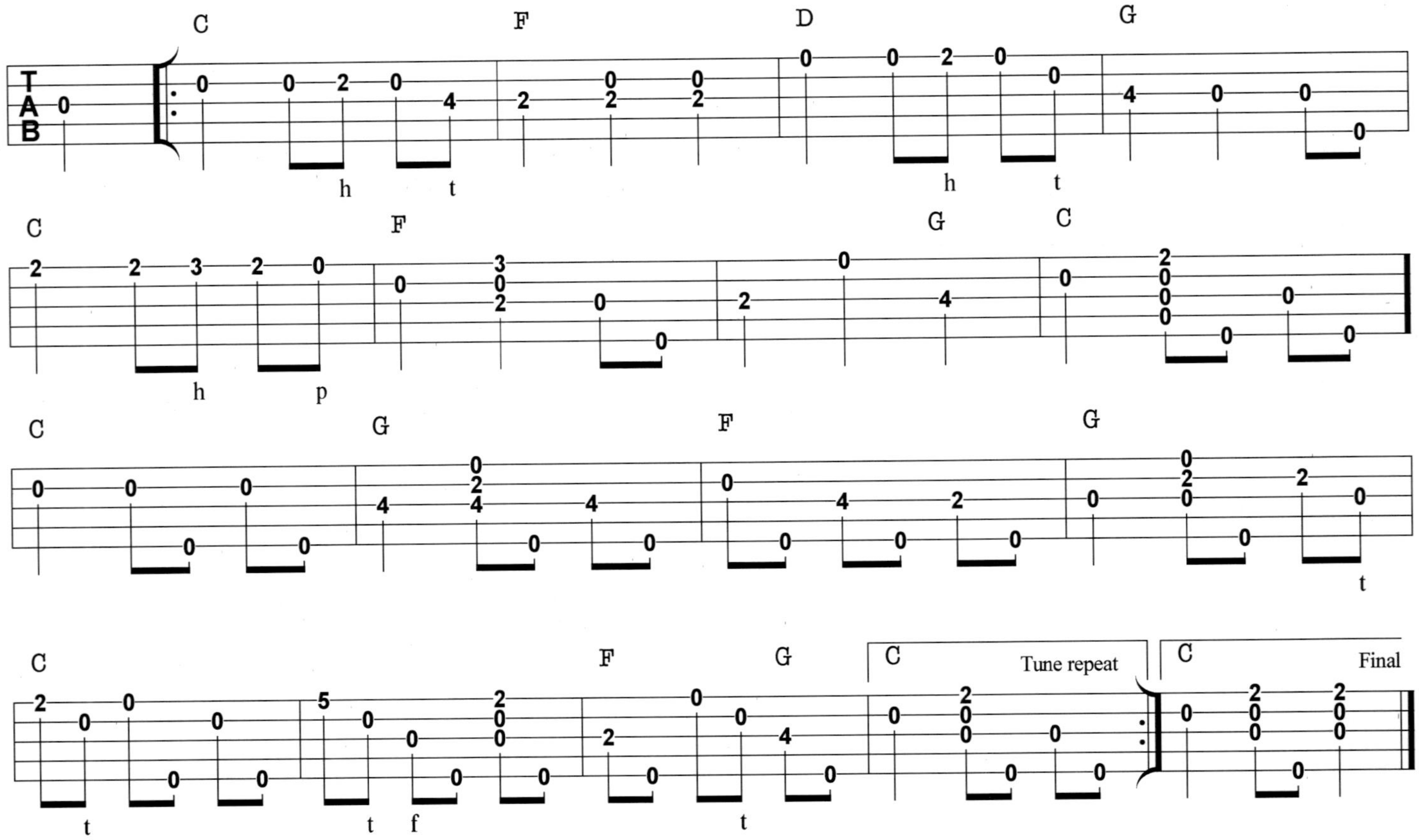

This tune works well in both double-C tuning and G tuning, so both versions are presented in this book.

28

We Wish You a Merry Christmas

(in G)

G Tuning
gDGBD

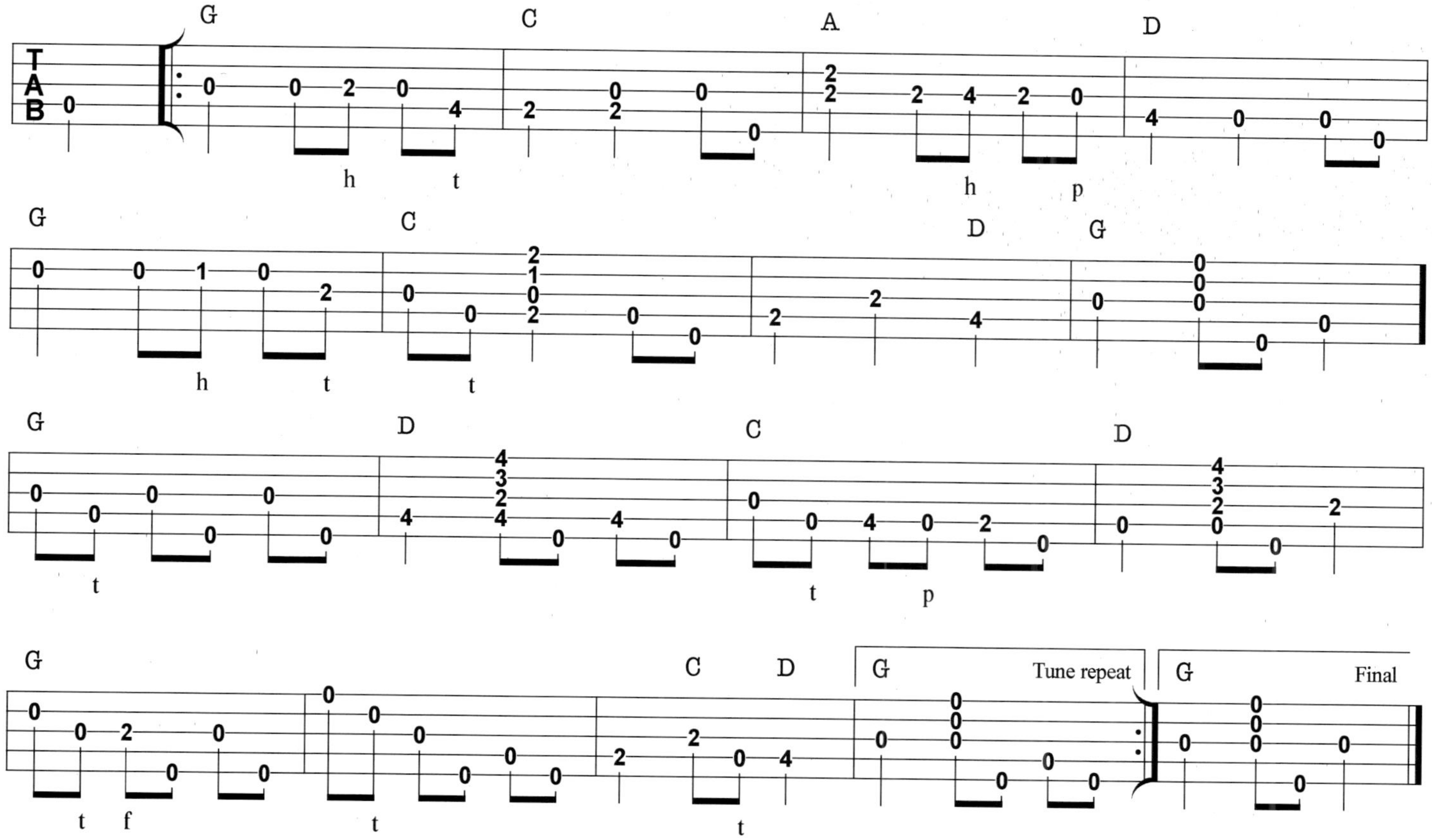

Take a bit of time with the D chords in the third line. I think you will find it worth the effort.

What Child Is This?

G-Modal Tuning
gDGCD

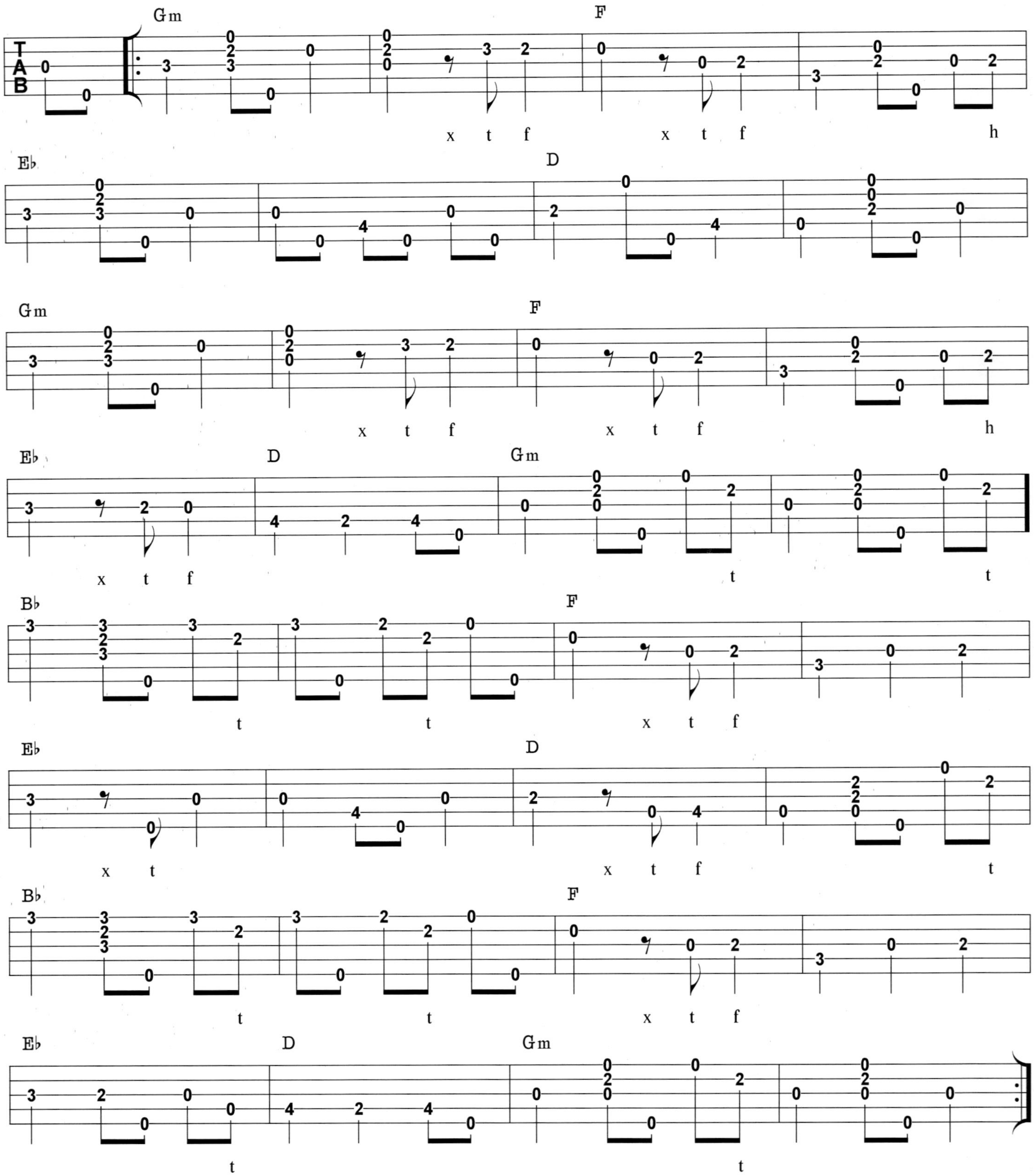

Auld Lang Syne

G Tuning
gDGBD

About the Author

Dan Levenson

Dan Levenson is an Appalachian native who has grown up with the music of that region. Today he is considered a respected master teacher and performer of both the clawhammer banjo & Appalachian-style fiddle. *Banjo NewsLetter's* R.D. Lunceford describes Dan as, "an interpreter, rather than a music re-creator". *Fiddler Magazine's* Bob Buckingham described him as, "an accomplished fiddler and ...one of the best clawhammer banjo players in the country." Ken Perlman has called him, "The Johnny Appleseed of the Banjo".

Dan performs and teaches regularly throughout the world including in England, Ireland, Israel and Brazil. He has taught at many music schools and camps including the John C. Campbell Folk School, Blue Ridge Old-Time Music Week at Mars Hill University, Maryland Banjo Academy, The Ozark Folk Center at Mountain View, AR, Banjo Camp North, The Rolland Fiddle Camp, and his own Clawcamp and Old-Time Music instructional weekends held at various locations throughout the country.

Dan has won awards on both clawhammer banjo and fiddle, including a 2017 Master Artist Award from Arizona's Southwest Folklife Alliance, first place at the 2005 Ohio Clawhammer Banjo Championship and Grand Champion at the 2010 Ajo, AZ Fiddle Contest.

Dan has 8 recordings of his own and is one of the most prolific authors of instructional and tune books for clawhammer banjo and fiddle with many Mel Bay publications to his name including: *Clawhammer Banjo from Scratch; Old Time Fiddle from Scratch* and the *Clawhammer Banjo Masters* series with co-author Bob Carlin (Kyle Creed, Wade Ward and Fred Cockerham & Tommy Jarrell volumes available). He is also a writer and editor for Banjo NewsLetter's "Old-Time Way".